CELEBRATING SERIES

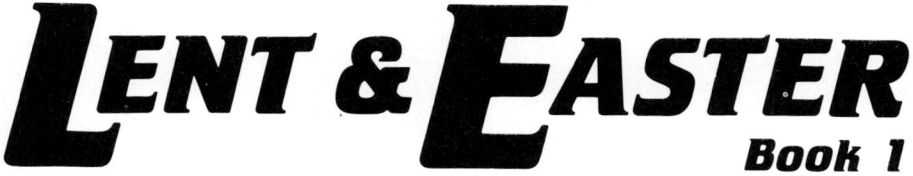

LENT & EASTER
Book 1

DONALD HILTON

FESTIVAL SERVICES for the Church Year

Other books by Donald Hilton

Boy into Man
Girl into Woman
Celebrating Series
Six Men and a Pulpit
Risks of Faith
Raw Materials of Faith
Results of Faith
After Much Discussion

Compiled by Donald Hilton

A Word in Season
Prayers for the Church Community
(with Roy Chapman)

Published by:
National Christian Education Council
Robert Denholm House
Nutfield
Redhill RH1 4HW

British Library Cataloguing-in-Publication Data:
Hilton, Donald *1932–*
   Celebrating Lent & Easter. – 2nd ed.
   Bk.1
   1. Christian church. Public worship – Rites
   I. Title II. National Christian Education Council
   264

ISBN 0-7197-0506-1

© 1987 Donald Hilton
Revised and reprinted 1991

Typeset by One and A Half Graphics, Redhill Surrey
Printed by Halstan & Co Ltd, Amersham, Buckinghamshire

PREFACE

This book contains four Festival Services; two for use on Sundays in Lent, one for Palm Sunday and the fourth for Easter Day. Beginning their life in a local church they have been written so that most, if not all age-groups in the church, can be involved.

The services will be found most useful where the Leader of worship gathers together those who work with the various age-groups in order to ensure full co-operation. The services should be altered and adapted in the light of local needs and opportunities.

Some churches may not want to include very young children in Lenten services but most of the services contain something which can interlock with their experience if only for a part of the service. At their best, Festival Services are celebrations by the whole church family, for the whole church family.

No place is given in the orders of service for either the Lord's Prayer or an offertory. These can be inserted according to local custom.

Donald Hilton

CONTENTS

3

POSITIVE LENT

Introduction

This service is designed for the Sunday before Lent begins, or the first Sunday in Lent. It explores Lent as a time for accepting new responsibilities rather than a demand for denial. Younger children are involved in the early part of the service and return later after carrying out tasks related to the service itself.

Preparation

The children under ten years of age, together with some adults will go to other rooms for part of the service in order, (1) to make pancakes, and (2) to prepare a Lent calendar. Appoint leaders for the two groups and decide which adults will join the children. Instructions for making pancakes and the calendar are given on page 11.

A simple leaflet with a few prayers appropriate for Lent will be given to every member of the congregation. Either search through books for appropriate prayers or form a small group to write them. Duplicate or photocopy enough copies. Remember to seek copyright permission where necessary.

Invite a responsible group in the church e.g. Deacons, Elders, Stewards or Church-meeting to make a list of ideas and plans about which their individual members of the church can be challenged as part of their response to Lent. (See suggestions given in the Order of Service.)

The Festival Service

Call to Worship

Open my lips, O Lord,
that my mouth may proclaim thy praise.
Thou hast no delight in sacrifice;
if I brought thee an offering, thou wouldst not accept it.
My sacrifice, O God, is a broken spirit;
a wounded heart, O God, thou wilt not despise.

(Psalm 51.15-17)

Hymn   Give to our God immortal praise

Prayer

Eternal God, the Father of our Lord Jesus Christ,
  you called Jesus to be your true servant,
  you were with him as he discovered his earthly task,
  you gave resources to stir spirit and imagination,
    and, so led, he accomplished your purpose.
Eternal God, our Father,
  we would become servants of yours in Christ's name,
  we seek help to discern our earthly tasks,
  we have become weakened in spirit and imagination..
    Lead us, so that we may accomplish your purpose.
Eternal God, Father of all peoples,
  you are calling the whole world to obedience,
  all humankind is caught up in your good intention,
  but we are lost in pettiness, and narrowness of spirit.
    Lead us all, eternal Father, until all that is created is brought
    within your purpose of love and truth.

Amen

Leader   Today is the first Sunday in Lent. *(alter if necessary)*. Five more Sundays and then the next will be Easter Day. That is the journey we begin to travel. We are not sure where the word Lent comes from. Perhaps from the old English word 'lente', meaning 'Spring', or an even older English word 'lencten' meaning 'to lengthen' for this is the time of the year when moving out of winter, the days grow longer.

Lent is forty working days long plus six Sundays. At the beginning of his ministry Jesus spent forty days and nights in a quiet place, with little food or water, to think about his life's work and what he believed

6

God wanted him to do. Lent has become our time to think about our discipleship and how we can best serve God.

Bible reading   Luke 4.1-13

Leader   To remember Jesus' hunger in the wilderness many Christians have used Lent as a time for fasting. Earlier, apart from Sundays, which are always celebration days, Christians ate no meat during Lent. Lent begins on a Wednesday so on the day before Lent began, always a Tuesday, all the meat and eggs were finished up. People in France and Spain called the Tuesday 'Mardi Gras' which means 'Fat Tuesday'; the day to eat up meat before Lent begins. In Britain a different practice developed. Pancakes were made to use up the eggs and fat. That's how Pancake Day started.

There is a different tradition in Greece. Children make Lent calendars to mark the weeks of Lent just as we have Advent calendars to mark the days before Christmas.

Two groups in the Church are going to follow these examples. One will make pancakes, the other a Lent calendar. The pancakes we'll eat at the end of the service, the calendar we'll use each Sunday until Easter,.

Hymn   Kum ba yah

The two groups of children and adults combined leave the church to complete their tasks.

Leader   'Denial' and 'giving things up' are a proper part of Christian discipleship. Unless it is trivialised by choosing only to give up things that don't really matter, or has become no more than an annual ritual, then using Lent as a time of self-discipline has its value.

But it can never be only by denial and ritual habits that we serve God. Amos and Micah, the great Old Testament prophets, represented God as pouring scorn on rituals that had lost their real meaning and thus blinded people to what was really happening in society.

Bible readings   *(use two different people)*
                     Amos 5.14-15 & 21-24
                     Micah 6.6-8

Story: Positive denial
Camillo Torres was born in Colombia. Colombia is a divided country. A score of families own the vast majority of the nation's wealth. Investigations have revealed that, because of malnutrition and the poor medical care of mothers, ten per cent of all babies die within a few days of birth. Tens of thousands of children die each year. More than a third

of the population is illiterate.

Camillo Torres was born into one of the few wealthy and influential families. But as well as being born with a silver spoon in his mouth, he was born with a conscience which later developed into a powerful instrument for change in his native land.

The Roman Catholic Church is strong in Colombia and Camillo Torres became a priest. As a lecturer and a chaplain at the University his faith deepened and his politics became more and more radical. 'Communist!' said his critics, among them members of the right wing Government of Colombia.

Torres put the political implications of his faith into practice. To landless peasants he gave away some of his own inherited land. He started an experimental farm to improve agricultural yield in an impoverished nation. He wrote – unsuccessfully – to some of the rich, land-owning families asking for a voluntary redistribution of wealth. Certainly, he brought together Christian and Communist elements in his nation arguing that, although very different in ideology, Christians and Communists are united in their care for starving people, and in a struggle for justice in society.

Criticised for such co-operation he could have echoed the puzzled comment of other Christian reformers:

When I feed the poor they tell me I am a Christian but when I ask why the poor are poor they tell me I am a Communist.

As a Roman Catholic priest the Mass – Catholic equivalent of our Communion Service – was central to Torres' life and worship.

Use the two readers to interject echoes of the Amos and Micah readings at this point in the story thus:

Amos reader Amos 5.21-22 and then verse 24
Micah reader Micah 6.8

Communion is the place where bread is shared; each person receives equally from the same loaf. In powerful symbolism the one cup is shared by all. Is such equality only for the act of worship, or is it for the whole of society? Faced by gross inequality and injustice from Monday to Saturday, does not Sunday Mass or Communion, with its symbols of sharing, become an empty ritual of the kind Amos and Micah condemned, in God's name?

Camillo Torres made what is for a Catholic priest an overwhelming act of self-denial. He stopped offering Mass. It was more than denial. It was a positive affirmation about human and religious values.

'I have stopped offering Mass,' Torres said, 'in order to live out the love of my neighbour in the temporal, economic and social orders. When my neighbour no longer has anything against me, and when the revolution has been completed, then I will offer Mass again.'

To all Christians Torres offers a challenge to ensure that the patterns of our worship speaks to the reality of human life. That is a Lenten challenge. He joins forces with Amos, Micah and many others to plead that we never lose ourselves in the life of the Church but show our discipleship in the everyday world. That is a Lenten plea.

If we hear the challenge and the plea then Lent is turned from denial into affirmation, and from a spirit of rejection to a positive acceptance of the will of God.

Hymn   Now quit your care *or*
          My dear Redeemer, and my Lord

Prayer
Father, our Lord and God, we offer this and every other act of worship we share in this church, to you.

May our shared prayer encourage shared action.

May our hearing of the words of the Bible bring us to obedience to your eternal Word in Jesus Christ.

May bread shared excite our concern for the hungry.

United in song may we seek harmony in the life of the Church and the life of the world.

May money given lead to given lives

and all to the end that your name is honoured in each day as in this Sunday praise.

Amen

Positive Lent
Arrange for a number of different people to announce the future plans and ideas to which members of the church can respond as an act of positive Lenten discipline. If children are still present include appropriate plans for them. The possibilities will depend on the life of the local church but might include;

- *Details of Lenten study groups, ecumenical or in the local church.*
- *Reviews of books to be read during Lent.*
- *Details of conferences in the Lent/Easter period.*
- *Appeal to collect for Christian Aid or other charities.*
- *Appeal to help in church or community projects.*
- *Invitation to gather information about a local, national or international need for later church action.*

- *A commitment to prayer using the prepared leaflet.*

Follow this part of the service with a period of silence for personal thoughts and commitment and conclude with the following meditation.

Meditation

God has created me to do him some definite service. He has committed some work to me which he has not committed to another. I have my mission. I may never know it in this world, but I shall be told it in the next.

I am a link in a chain, a bond of connection between persons. He has not created me for naught.

I shall do good. I shall do his work. I shall be an angel of peace, a preacher of truth in my own place, while not intending it, if I do but keep his commandments.

Therefore will I trust in him. Wherever, whatever I am, I can never be thrown away. If I am in sickness, my sickness may serve him; in perplexity, my perplexity may serve him; if I am in sorrow, my sorrow may serve him.

He does nothing in vain. He knows what he is about. He may take away my friends, he may throw me among strangers. He may make me feel desolate, make my spirits sink, hide my future from me ... still ... he knows what he is about.

(Cardinal Newman)

Hymn   O Thou who camest from above

The two groups return during the hymn. The pancake group distributes pieces of pancake to all the congregation (or better still invite them to a pancake party after the service); the calendar group presents the calendar to the Leader, explains its purpose and asks that it should be left in a prominent position and used in Family worship on each Sunday in Lent. The prayer leaflets are distributed to the congregation. The Leader withdraws the first feather from the calendar.

Bible reading   *indicated by the Lent calendar (unless the service is being used on the Sunday before Lent)*

Prayer   *read by the congregation from the leaflet*

Hymn   Surrounded by a world of need *or*
Tell out, my soul, the greatness of the Lord

Benediction.

The Pancake Group

The following recipe will make about a dozen normal size pancakes. Use a smaller pan if you want to provide complete pancakes; otherwise larger ones can be cut before being served.

4oz (100gm) plain flour
a pinch of salt
2 large eggs
two tablespoons melted butter
7 fl oz (200 ml) milk mixed with 3 fl oz (75 ml) water
A little extra butter for cooking the pancakes

Sieve flour and salt into mixing bowl. Break two eggs into it. Whisk the eggs incorporating the flour. Gradually add milk/water. Whisk until all is smooth. Immediately before cooking, stir in the melted butter.

To cook, melt a teaspoonful of butter in the pan, swirl to cover pan and remove excess butter. Get the pan hot and, for normal sized pancakes add about 2 tablespoons of the batter to the pan. Swirl to cover pan base. Each pancake takes about 30 seconds to cook. Some pancakes could be made in advance, wrapped, refrigerated and then reheated on the Sunday either in an oven or on a pan of simmering water.

The Calendar Group

Scrub a large potato clean. Pierce a hole through it using a skewer or knitting needle. Thread a piece of string or ribbon through the hole and make a knot in the end so that the potato can be suspended. A small circle of thick card between the knot and the potato prevents the string slipping through.

Make seven feathers by cutting out a feather shape in thick card and glueing it to a cocktail stick. Write one of the following bible references on each feather and mark the feathers 1-7 to show the weeks in Lent. Stick the seven feathers into the potato.

Bible references:

First week: Hebrews 2.14-16   Second week: Luke 19.41-48
Third week: Luke 9.18-27   Fourth week: Luke 9.28-36
Fifth week: John 12.20-32   Sixth week: Matthew 21.1-9
                Seventh week: Matthew 28.1-7

A MAN FOR ALL PEOPLE

Introduction

Jesus was born into a divided and prejudiced world. Slavery was common. Women were second class citizens. Children were virtually non-people. The Romans felt superior in their military power; the Jews felt themselves racially superior. Greeks despised barbarians. The testimony of the early Church was that Jesus bridged these divisions and spoke to everyone. He was a man for all people. This service uses biblical and contemporary evidence to explore that conviction.

Preparation

Select the readers needed for the service noting the different way they are used, and that both women and men are required.

Prepare actors for the dramatic reading.

Arrange for the group of children who will play games.

Ask the World Church or Missionary Committee in your church to plan a small exhibition showing work across the world.

Prepare materials and leaders to help the children produce the flags of the nations. See page 18 for details of some flags.

The Festival Service

Call to Worship

God abides in men,
because Christ has put on
the nature of man, like a garment,
and worn it to his own shape.
He has put on everyone's life.
He has fitted himself to the little child's dress,
to the shepherd's coat of sheepskin,
to the workman's coat,
to the King's red robes,
to the snowy loveliness of the wedding garment,

and to the drab
of the sad, simple battle dress.
Christ has put on man's nature,
and given him back his humanness,
worn to the shape
of limitless love,
and warm from the touch
of his life.

(Caryll Houselander)

Hymn A man there lived in Galilee

Prayer

Lord Jesus Christ, child of Mary and Joseph,
> born in Bethlehem, brought up in Nazareth, speaking to the crowds
> in Galilee, entering Jerusalem on a donkey and dying outside a city
> wall, you knew but one time and one country. Life and birth, and the
> purposes of God anchor you in history.

Lord Jesus Christ, Son of the Father,
> by God's good purpose you broke the bonds of time, leapt the walls
> of place, and pioneered the journey into the future. All ages and people
> have known you and eternity sings your glory.

Lord Jesus Christ, Word of God,
> you fill all time and place. Corner stone and foundation of the universe
> you were at the beginning and are at the end. Your purpose fulfills
> all things and your love is at the heart of life itself.

> With people of every time and place we offer adoration and praise.

Amen

Reader 1 Take one impulsive, sometimes rash young workman and
introduce him to an accountant. Call others to the group and make sure
the generation gap is well represented. Bring in a man steeped in radical
politics and ready to stir things up. Ensure a good mixture of people with
both idealism and down to earth commonsense and add at least one
person whose integrity is questionable. What do you have? A powder
keg of human personality ready to blow up at the first moment - or a
group of twelve disciples bonded together in common allegiance to Jesus
Christ and ready to turn the world upside down?

Reader 2 The group of disciples are a living parable in the ministry of
Jesus. Jesus Christ was a man for all people, with the ability to hold
together a diverse group because he spoke to the heart of each one.

13

The disciples were a double symbol - symbol of the social and political divisions of the time of Jesus, and symbol of the community Jesus could create out of such divisions.

Reader 1   The divisions in society were even deeper, and bred oppression and injustice. Slaves, sold as possessions were divided from freemen, rich from poor. The Romans were hated by the Jews, the Jews despised by the Romans. Women were second-class citizens, and children counted as nothing. Female babies were often cast out at birth, or deliberately maimed so that they could be better employed as beggars. People suffering from leprosy were ejected from society and prevented from approaching any habitation.

Reader 2   This was the world at the time of Jesus.

Reader 1   This was the world to which Jesus came and accepted the role of servant; servant of God, and servant of all God's children - a man for all people.

A man for those who are ill

Leader   In the days of Jesus the sick could be discounted. People believed that suffering was directly due to human sin and was thus deserved. So the blind, those with leprosy, and those crippled, had no cause to complain - they had brought it on themselves by their sin, or else it was the legacy of the sin of their parents. From Jesus came flashing new insight. Using two recent disasters, one of human oppression, one of sheer accident, he broke the idea of inevitable connection between sin and suffering.

Reader 1   Luke 13.1-5

Reader 2   Dramatic reading. Read Luke 8.1-4. *Act out the story in modern dress with two men representing Jesus and the man with leprosy, and about six or eight people representing the crowd.*

Verse 1: Jesus enters with several people.

Verse 2: A man enters wearing a blanket over his usual clothes. He approaches Jesus very tentatively. The other people draw back in fear. As the man with leprosy slowly gets closer to Jesus, who stands firm, the crowds show fear and displeasure and at least one runs away.

Verses 3-4: Jesus touches the man who kneels. After a moments stillness the man throws off his blanket and stands up with evident joy. Some of the crowd approach to congratulate the man, others remain hesitant.

Prayer

Father God, we praise you for all those who, inspired by Jesus, have given themselves in the service of the sick.

We remember Peter, who healed a crippled man by the Gate Beautiful, symbol of all healing in the early Church.

We remember the medieval monks, symbol of all who have provided shelter and care for the sick and dying.

We remember Father Damien, founding a haven for those with leprosy, and symbol of all who have risked their own health for others.

We remember Albert Schweitzer, building a hospital in Africa, and symbol of all medical missionaries.

We remember Mother Teresa, working in India, and becoming a symbol of all those who have seen Christ in the eyes of the neglected.

We give thanks for doctors, nurses, dentists, surgeons, the architects of our National Health Service, the planners and administrators, symbol of all who look for fullness of life and health for all people.

May the example of Jesus Christ inspire them.

Amen

A man for children

Leader We have a letter that comes to us from the time of Jesus. It was written by Alis, the wife of a labourer called Hilarion who had left home to find work. Alis was expecting a baby and wrote to her husband asking for news and telling him of the coming child. She received a letter in reply.

'Hilarion to his wife Alis, very many greetings. Know that we are still in Alexendria. Do not be anxious. As soon as we receive our pay I will send it to you. If by chance you bear a child and it is a boy, rear him. If it is a girl, cast it out ...'

The practice was commonplace. All children were a burden, girls a greater burden because they would never be wage-earning. Life was cheap and the lives of children, cheapest of all. That was the world to which Jesus came.

Children's games *With a piano playing quietly a group of little children come to the front of the church and play simple games e.g. dancing in a ring, Oranges and Lemons. Over the top of the music read the following:*

Reader 1 Luke 18.15-17

Reader 2

Children are a gift to the Church. The Lord of the Church sets them in the midst of the Church, today as in Galilee, not as objects of benevolence, nor even as recipients of instruction, but in the last analysis as patterns of discipleship. The Church that does not accept children unconditionally into its fellowship is depriving those children of what is rightfully theirs, but the deprivation such a Church will itself suffer is far more grave.

(Child in the Church)

Hymn *Churches that practise infant baptism might choose a baptismal hymn e.g. Lord Jesus, once a child; other churches might choose a hymn relating to childhood. At the close of the hymn the children move to another room. There they produce flags of several nations, by colouring thick card. Fastened to canes these will be used towards the end of the service as a major part of exploring the ministry of Jesus as 'A man for all nations'.*

A man for the other 50 per cent

A woman reads

Florence Nightingale wrote:

I would have given the church my head, my hand, my heart. She would not have them. She did not know what to do with them. She told me to go back and do crochet in my mother's drawing room; or, if I were tired of that, to marry and look well at the head of my husband's table. 'You may go to Sunday School if you like it', she said. But she gave me no training even for that. She gave me neither work to do for her, nor education for it.

A man reads

When his wife was given a garden fork as a Christmas present, Rupert Davies, a Methodist minister wrote:

When Adam delved and Eve span
Woman, no doubt, was less than man.
When Eve begins to delve as well,
How can folks Eve from Adam tell?
So Adam must his pride maintain
By boasting a superior brain.
But this false claim is knocked for six
When Eve goes into politics.

So what is left for Adam still
Except to steal and rape and kill?
Unless you think - and you'd be right
That Eve and Adam in God's sight
Are equal partners in the strife
Of building up the common life.

A woman reads

Mother Julian, the fourteenth century Norwich mystic wrote:

I saw that God rejoices that he is our father, and God rejoices that
he is our mother, and God rejoices that he is our very husband, and
our soul his beloved wife. And Christ rejoices that he is our brother,
and Jesus rejoices that he is our saviour. These are five great joys, as
I see it, which he wills us to delight in - praising him, thanking him,
loving him and blessing him for ever.

Reading   Mark 3.31-35

Prayer

Grant, eternal God, that the rich gifts you have poured into your church
through those you have called to be its members, may be honoured and
wisely used. May gifts of gentleness and strength unite in service. May
cool logic and spontaneous insight join in commitment. May the gifts,
symbolised by motherhood and fatherhood but present in each of us,
be released in us all. Thus, joined in community, may all your people
serve your Kingdom.

Amen

A man for all nations

Hymn   Saviour, quicken many nations

Leader   Jesus was a Jew; so were all the first disciples. It was not until
after the resurrection and the creation of the early Church that the issue
arose, 'Can non-Jews join the Church?' As they looked back on the life
and ministry of Jesus it became clear to the Church that in accepting the
Gentiles they were being faithful to the Gospel of Christ. They remem-
bered the centurion's servant, the woman from Canaan, and the time
that certain Greek people approached Jesus.

Reading   John 12.20-26

Invite a small group of people to walk around the exhibition produced by the

World Church or Missionary Committee. Comment on the pictures. Draw out the significance of the worldwide nature of the Church. Ensure that everyone in the church can hear what is said.

Hymn The whole wide world for Jesus
During this hymn the children return and process around the church carrying the flags of the nations.

Prayer

Lord Jesus Christ, the world is in great need of your message and love. There is misunderstanding between young and old, argument between nations, a great divide between the rich and the poor, a hurtful gap between the hungry and the well-fed, and mistrust between workers and management in industry. We need someone to show us how divisions can be healed, gaps closed, and reconciliation achieved.

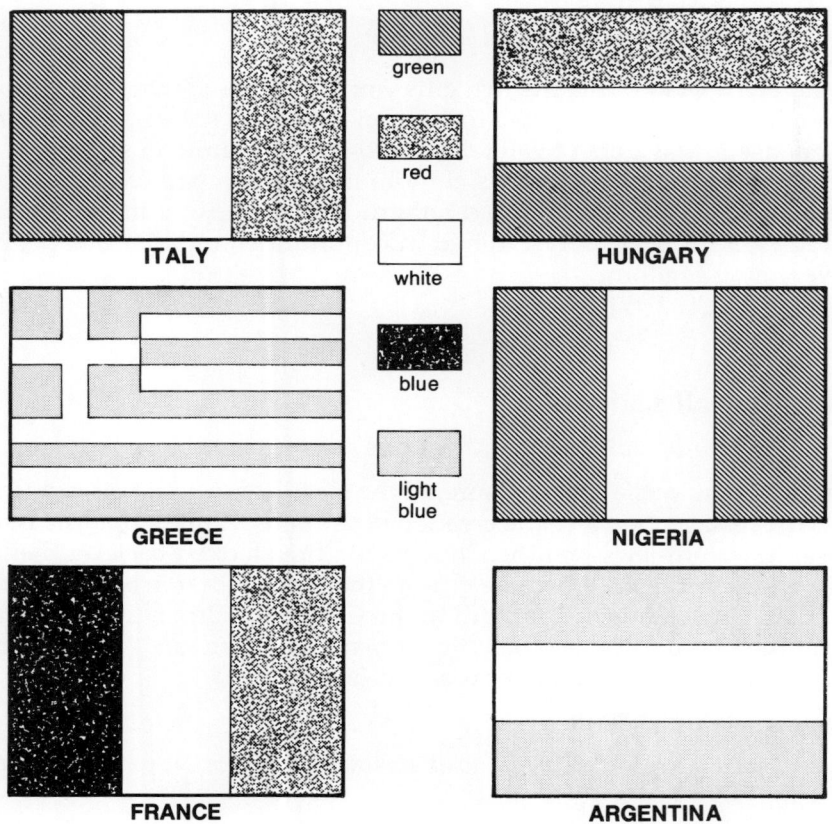

We hear your teaching and we see your life. The stories of your birth show us workmen – shepherds, and wise men worshipping together; your group of disciples show us men of differing ability and belief united in service; your death evoked a response which cut across the usual division of Jew and Gentile; and the gift of your Spirit created a new community able to step across ancient barriers with gaiety and ease.

Lord Jesus Christ, we need someone to come and help us in our world today. From your teaching and your life we believe you are the one to do it. Come, Lord Jesus.

(Prayers for the Church Community)

Hymn   Head of the Church, our risen Lord

Benediction

MAN OF DESTINY

Introduction

This is a service for Palm Sunday. From the pinnacle which this day represents we look back to the ministry of Jesus to see him as healer, teacher and friend. With that in mind we celebrate Palm Sunday itself and then move on through Holy Week reflecting on the events of each day. We halt at Saturday with a mere hint at the victory of Easter Day.

We cannot be sure about the precise days on which all the various events took place. We can safely place the Last Supper on the Thursday and the Cross on Friday but the questioning (here allocated to Tuesday) went on all week and even the Gospel writers are unsure about when the Cleansing of the Temple took place. This service tends towards Mark's reading of events.

Preparation

Collect pictures of Jesus the healer, teacher, and friend and mount them in such a way that they can be carried in procession. Suitable pictures can be found in New Testament Pictures for Today and An Easter Frieze both available from the National Christian Education Council. Decide at which points in the church the procession can pause. The three processions could be made up of three different groups of children, or the same group can form all three processions, leaving each set of pictures on display at the front of the church before forming the next procession.

Prepare a large eight-sheet calendar. Leave the first sheet blank. The second sheet should be marked PALM SUNDAY, and successive sheets be given the days of the week from MONDAY to SATURDAY inclusive. The calendar and lettering must be large enough for everyone in church to read it. One person will turn the sheets, and can also read the sections of the Bible given at those points. You will also need a second reader and a choral-reading group. Prepare the people who will mime Luke 20.19-26 and the two involved in the dialogue between Procula and Longinus. The mime actors should be in modern dress but Procula and Longinus as a first century lady, and a centurion.

This Festival Service was first published in *Partners in Learning*.

The Festival Service

Opening sentences Jesus took the Twelve aside and said, 'We are now going up to Jerusalem; and all that was written by the prophets will come true for the Son of Man. He will be handed over to the foreign power. He will be mocked, maltreated, and spat upon. They will flog him and kill him. And on the third day he will rise again.' They understood nothing of this; they did not grasp what he was talking about; its meaning was concealed from them.

Luke 18.31-34

Leader We stand with the disciples. We have heard the words of Jesus but have not fully understood. We have shared many years in which Lent has led to Palm Sunday, Palm Sunday to Good Friday, and then Easter Day, but have still not fully understood the meaning of it all. This morning we make that journey again. Pray that God will help us to understand more fully the message of his Son.

Hymn Praise to the Holiest in the height

Prayer

It is the baby we remember; the baby who was just like any other baby and yet was God indeed.

It is the boy we remember, growing up like every other boy, knowing the joy and pain of growth and slowly learning more of himself and of God.

It is the young man we remember; sometimes angry, sometimes uncertain, sometimes knowing, sometimes searching, but always holding the presence of God in his life and standing alongside ordinary people in love and compassion.

It is Jesus we remember; may the memory refresh us and bring us closer to you, O God, with thankful adoration and grateful praise.

(Prayers for the Church Community)

Leader The events of Palm Sunday claim our attention, and they will take us on to the final week in the life of Jesus. But before that we remind ourselves of all that has gone before in the life of Jesus when women and men welcomed him, loved him and received his gifts and help.

The first group of children and young people process around the church to very quiet background music displaying pictures of 'Jesus the healer' They pause at several agreed places so that the whole congregation can see the pictures. As they process the choral-reading group announces 'Jesus the healer' and reads

Mark 1.21-27 (see page 27). If three different groups of children are processing they should stand or sit near the front as their procession comes to an end, ready for the Palm Sunday procession later.

A second procession displays pictures of 'Jesus the teacher', pausing as before and then standing at the front. As they process the choral-group reads Matthew 5.3-10 (see page 27).

Hymn Tell me the stories of Jesus
(Omit the verses relating to Palm Sunday and Good Friday)

A third procession displays pictures of 'Jesus the friend' e.g. any pictures of Jesus in conversation or in a one-to-one relationship; the choral group reads John 15.11-17 (see page 28)

Prayers *spoken by two members of the choral group.*
1 We thank God for the friendship of Jesus
    We have friends. Thank you for them Lord.
    But some of them forget us, and you never do;
    and some of them are unkind to us, and you never are;
    some of them are real friends one day, and act like enemies the
    next, but you are always the same.
    Thank you, Lord Jesus, for your unfailing friendship.
    Help us to be as loyal to you as you are to us.

(Prayers for the Church Community)

2 Confident of the friendship of Jesus we pray for others
    Lord Jesus, you do not call us servants; you call us friends and
        that is good news indeed!
    When people are depressed may they hear the good news
        of your compassion
    When people are anxious may they learn of your care.
    When people are afraid may they know that nothing can
        separate them from your love.
    May your love disperse anger and hatred and renew
        love and faith so that, being your friends, we may
        be friends with each other.

(Prayers for the Church Community)

Leader Jesus, healer, teacher, and friend. These are the pictures we can take into this coming week as we watch him walk through its days, ready to meet whatever confronts him. As we begin this week, we already know its sadness and ultimate joy. Good Friday will come with its pain, and so will Easter Day with its victory. Jesus and his disciples did not know that they walked into a week of uncertainty, not knowing what any day would bring. We can only walk with them if we carry the gifts of imagination and close sympathy. And now we begin the journey ... *The person appointed turns back the blank sheet on the calendar to reveal the words PALM SUNDAY.*

Hymn   All glory, laud, and honour
As the hymn begins the children from the processions put down their pictures and pick up small branches or homemade paper palm branches and process around the church again. At the end of the hymn the young children can leave the church, whilst the older children move to seats in the congregation. As the congregation sits the person appointed changes the calendar to MONDAY and reads Mark 11.15-17.

Making palm branches

Use thin green card for the palm leaves. Do not cut right to the middle.

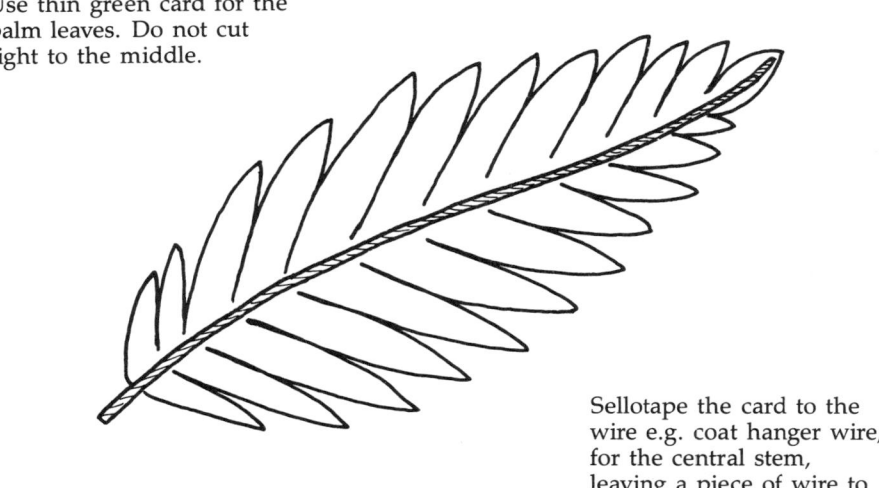

Sellotape the card to the wire e.g. coat hanger wire, for the central stem, leaving a piece of wire to hold.

Second Reader The life of the temple received its judgment. It had misunderstood its role. That is a constant danger for the Church in all ages. It is also our danger today. A group of Christians expressed it thus:

The fundamental principle, which we share with other Christians, is that Church life must be so ordered as most fully to express the Lordship of Christ, and enable the Church to fulfil its mission in the world at each and every place and time. In part we know already what this means. But we know, too, that the Church must constantly look to the judgment of God upon its own life. Where its thought and practice are reformed and renewed in love and obedience, answering God's grace, true life for the Church will be re-born.

(from A Declaration of Faith by the Congregational Church in England & Wales)

The calendar is changed to TUESDAY and Luke 20.19-26 is read to a mime i.e.

verses 19-20	Three or four people mime an agitated conversation off centre. They beckon to two others and whisper instructions. The two move to the centre and so does another actor representing Jesus.
verses 21-23	The two approach Jesus with obsequious gestures and bows. Jesus is calm. The others, off centre, look smug.
verses 24-25	Jesus holds out his hand. They reach into their pockets for a coin and hand it to him. Jesus examines it carefully and points to Caesars's head. Those off centre express angry frustration.
verse 26	The two men return to the others who have been watching the incident. With angry resignation they leave. Jesus walks away sadly.

The calendar is changed to WEDNESDAY and Matthew 26.14-16 is read.

Second Reader

He could not live with himself.
His regrets were too great to be borne.
He committed suicide.
I find myself sympathising with Judas, Lord.
Had he wanted to force your hand?
Had he heard you talk so much about God's kingdom that he wanted some divine vindication?
Did he feel that by putting you on the spot, God-in-you would be bound to act decisively, dramatically?

Perhaps he had even prayed about it and thought about it, only to see his whole scheme backfire in his face ...
He is everyman who has to live or die with his past.
Strengthen me to come to terms with myself and my actions in the light of your death and your resurrection.
'There is nothing in all creation that can separate us from the love of God in Christ Jesus our Lord'.

(Rex Chapman)

The calendar is changed to THURSDAY. Then:

Either Matthew 26.26-29 is read, during which the Leader breaks small, whole loaves to pass among the congregation for each to take a piece and eat. (This would not be a Communion Service but a dramatic representation of the reading.) A music voluntary may be needed if the distribution takes longer than the reading.

Or The Leader conducts a normal Communion Service.

Hymn   When I survey the wondrous cross

During the hymn the calendar is changed to FRIDAY. Then:

Either Matthew 27.45-50 is read:

or two people dressed in first century clothes read the following:

PROCULA	Centurion, were you at the killing of that teacher today?
LONGINUS	Yes, lady.
PROCULA	Tell me about his death.
LONGINUS	It is hardly fit hearing for you, my lady ...
PROCULA	Do not tell it all, then, but tell me what he said.
LONGINUS	The people were mocking him at first, and he prayed to God to forgive them. He said: 'Father, forgive them, for they know what what they do ...'
PROCULA	Was he suffering much?
LONGINUS	No, lady. He wasn't a strong man. The scourging must have nearly killed him. I thought he was dead by noon, and then suddenly he began to sing in a loud voice that he was giving back his spirit to God. I looked to see God come to take him. He died singing. Truly, lady, that man was the Son of God, if one may say that ...
PROCULA	What do you think the man believed, centurion?
LONGINUS	He believed he was God, they say.
PROCULA	What do you think of that claim?
LONGINUS	If a man believes anything up to the point of dying on a cross for it, he will find others to believe it.

PROCULA	Do you believe it?
LONGINUS	He was a fine young fellow, my lady; not past middle age. And he was all alone, and defied all the Jews and all the Romans, and, when we had done with him, he was a poor broken-down thing, dead on the cross.
PROCULA	Do you think he is dead?
LONGINUS	No, lady, I don't.
PROCULA	Then where is he?
LONGINUS	Let loose in the world, lady, where neither Roman nor Jew can stop his truth.

(John Masefield)

The calendar is changed to SATURDAY

Leader Saturday. For the disciples, Saturday was the day of anguish which would have no end to it. Life was finished. Jesus was dead. The disciples were as good as dead. They descended into hell. There would be no Sunday.

For us, knowing the end with the beginning, it is the waiting day. God will do his glorious and victorious best. He always does.

In prayer we wait with Christ and his disciples.

Provide at least a full minutes silence

Prayer

The sufferings of the world are yours, eternal Christ. You bear the shame of mankind as though it was your own.

The agony of rejection is yours, eternal Christ. You faced human rejection throughout your life and, on the cross, you felt yourself to be rejected even by God.

Out of your dereliction comes our hope. You descended to the depths to raise us to the heights.

The glory is yours, and the victory and you give both to us as though they were ours by right.

Come, Lord Jesus Christ. We who begin to tread this holy week await your coming.

Hymn Christ is the world's true light

Dismissal The world awaits you and Christ is there before you. Take this week that God has given. Watch and wait with Christ until the purposes of God are fulfilled.

Amen

Choral readings (see page 21)

Mark 1.21-27

VOICE 1	They came to Capernaum, and on the Sabbath he went to the synagogue and began to teach.
ALL	The people were astounded at his teaching, for, unlike the doctors of the law, he taught with a note of authority.
VOICE 1	Now there was a man in the synagogue possessed by an unclean spirit. He shrieked:
VOICE 2	What do you want with us, Jesus of Nazareth? Have you come to destroy us? I know who you are - the Holy One of God.
VOICE 1	Jesus rebuked him:
VOICE 3	Be silent and come out of him.
VOICE 1	And the unclean spirit threw the man into convulsions and with a loud cry left him. They were all dumbfounded and began to ask one another:
ALL	What is this? A new kind of teaching! He speaks with authority. When he gives orders, even the unclean spirits submit.

Matthew 5.3-10

VOICE 1	How blest are those who know their need of God;
ALL	the kingdom of God is theirs.
VOICE 2	How blest are the sorrowful;
ALL	they shall find consolation.
VOICE 3	How blest are those of a gentle spirit;
ALL	they shall have the earth for their possession.
VOICE 1	How blest are those who hunger and thirst to see right prevail;
ALL	they shall be satisfied.
VOICE 2	How blest are those who show mercy;
ALL	mercy shall be shown to them.
VOICE 3	How blest are those whose hearts are pure;
ALL	they shall see God.
VOICE 1	How blest are the peacemakers;
ALL	God shall call them his sons.
	How blest are those who have suffered persecution for the cause of right;

VOICE 2	The Kingdom of Heaven is theirs.
John 15.11-17	*Divide the group into two sections*
SECTION 1	Jesus said: I have spoken thus to you, so that my joy may be in you, and your joy complete. This is my commandment: love one another, as I have loved you.
SECTION 2	There is no greater love than this, that a man should lay down his life for his friends
SECTION 1	You are my friends if you do what I command you. I call you servants no longer; a servant does not know what his master is about. I have called you friends because I have disclosed to you everything that I heard from my Father.
SECTION 2	You did not choose me: I chose you. I appointed you to go on and bear fruit, fruit that shall last; so that my Father may give you all that you ask in my name.
SECTION 1	This is my commandment to you: love one another.

THINE BE THE GLORY

Introduction
This service affirms the glory of God experienced in creation, art, music, science, all human experience, and chiefly in the life, death and rising of Jesus Christ. It is appropriate for adults and older children, especially if the older children share in some of the readings, and in the Glory Group. Younger children can leave for their own worship at the point indicated.

Preparation
Approach members of the congregation, and use the public library to find pictures of various paintings or statues which portray Jesus Christ or interpret the nature of God. In small congregations these can be handed around, in larger ones enough pictures will be needed to display them around the church so that everyone can see at least one. There are likely to be more flowers in church on Easter Day than usual. Invite the arrangers to produce arrangements on Easter themes e.g. 'Joy' (using bright spring flowers) or 'Glory' (using bold colours and perhaps trumpet flowers such as lilies. Local flower groups often welcome an invitation to be involved.

Invite a group of people of various ages to be the 'Glory Group' and read the affirmations that occur as a chorus throughout the service. These affirmations form the prayers in the service. Three other readers are needed. The Glory Group and the group of three readers should remain in one place throughout the service.

The Festival Service

Call to worship
First voice Jesus looked up to heaven and said: 'Father, the hour has come. Glorify thy Son, that the Son may glorify thee. For thou hast made him sovereign over all mankind, to give eternal life to all whom thou hast given him. This is eternal life: to know thee who alone art truly God, and Jesus Christ whom thou hast sent.

(John 17.1-3)

Second voice

> While we deliberate, God reigns;
> When we decide wisely, God reigns;
> When we decide foolishly, God reigns;
> When we serve him in humble loyalty, he reigns;
> When we serve him self-assertively, he reigns
> When we rebel and seek to withhold our service,
> He reigns; the Alpha and the Omega,
> Which was, and which is, and which is to come,
> The Almighty.

(William Temple)

Hymn   Thine be the glory, risen conquering Son

Prayer

> The glory is yours, eternal God.
>> When voices are raised in adoration and praise,
>> When Easter joy fills every heart,
>> When your triumph over death is proclaimed,
>>> All glory is yours.
> The glory is yours, eternal God.
>> When the shadow of a cross darkens life,
>> When in neglect the voice of praise is silent,
>> When people live as though you were no more,
>>> All glory still is yours
> The glory is yours, eternal God.
>> Now on this day,
>> Now in this church
>> Now in our hearts,
>>> The glory is yours. Amen

Leader   There is a mighty chorus to sing the praise of God. Creation testifies to God's great power. Through all ages men and women have glorified God with art and music, poetry and science. The quiet place of the human heart and the Easter experience cry aloud at God's glory. This morning we share that universal experience and celebrate God's glory and power.

LET CREATION GLORIFY GOD

First reader   Psalm 19.1-4

Second reader   Exodus 3.1-6

Third reader

      ... nothing's small;

No lily; muffled hum of summer bee,
But finds some coupling with the spinning stars;
No pebble at your foot, but proves a sphere;
No chaffinch, but implies a cherubim;
      Earth's crammed with heaven,
And ever common bush afire with God;
But only he who sees takes off his shoes,
The rest sit round it and pluck blackberries.

                        (Elizabeth Barrett Browning)

Hymn Welcome, happy morning! age to age shall say *– (139) CP)*

Affirmation *(The Glory group)*

      Thine be the glory, Creator Lord.
      Glory seen
      in mysterious impenetrable night and in morning light,
      in the vast reaches of space and the tiny atom,
      in hills that have for ages stood and in ephemeral time,
      in intricate flowers and in the sweep of the broad meadow,
      in rushing waterfall and silent sea,
      and in humankind, made in your image.
      Thine be the glory, Creator Lord.

The younger children can leave at this point and take further the theme of God's glory in creation by creating a Worship Table in their own room using arrangements of flowers, objects such as shells and stones, and pictures of the life of Jesus.

Leader LET ART AND SCIENCE GLORIFY GOD

Invite the congregation to look at the flower arrangements around the church, and at the pictures of paintings and statues etc. The leader or someone else should reflect on one or two of the pictures and suggest how the artist's skill has been used to show the significance of some aspect of the life of Christ. A flower arranger could comment briefly on an arrangement.

First reader A young worker glorifies God:

      Can we not say to the young apprentice who has just learnt the use of a high precision lathe, and is thrilled at his new ability to use so apparently heavy and bulky a machine to prepare a piece of metal to a given shape with an accuracy of one ten-thousandth of an inch, that God is equally thrilled, and that this sheer joy in the situation is not wholly different from that of the angels who behold God's glory and rejoice?

(Charles Coulson)

Affirmation *(The Glory Group)*

Thine be the glory, Lord of Beauty, Wonder, Truth.
Glory seen in the patterns of creation, colour on colour,
    in the gifts of human skill and ingenuity,
    in architecture, painting, sculpture, and design
    in computer science,technology, and human inventiveness,
Thine be the glory, Lord of Beauty, Wonder, Truth.

Leader LET MUSIC GLORIFY GOD

Either the church choir can sing a anthem, or records be used to play music that speaks of God's glory e.g. 'The Hallelujah Chorus' from Handel's 'Messiah' or the 'Sanctus' from Lloyd Webber's 'Requiem Mass'.

Leader CHRIST THE LORD REVEALS GOD'S GLORY

Hymn Christ the Lord is risen today *(c P 145)*

First reader John 20.1,11-18

Second reader Hebrews 1.1-4

Affirmation *(The Glory group)*

Thine be the glory, Lord Jesus Christ.
    Glory seen in simplicity in a Bethlehem manger,
    in a child advancing in wisdom and in favour with God and men,
    in works of healing, love and compassion,
    in teaching to stir the heart and invite obedience,
    in self-giving, even to a cross,
    and in resurrection splendour.
Thine be the glory, Lord Jesus Christ.

Hymn Good Christian men, rejoice and sing *(c P. 149)*

Leader AND LET US, ALL WE ARE AND HOPE TO BE, GLORIFY GOD

First reader Romans 8.14-17

Second reader

    If you believe that Christ has risen from the dead,
        you must believe also that you yourselves have likewise risen
            with him ...

And if you believe yourself dead with Christ,
  you must believe that you will also live with him;
And if you believe that Christ is dead to sin, and lives to God,
  you too must be dead to sin, and alive to God.

(Origen)

Third reader In John Masefield's poem 'The Everlasting Mercy' a converted sinner finds every aspect of his life illuminated by God's glory.

O glory of the lighted mind.
How dead I'd been, how dumb, how blind.
The station brook, to my new eyes,
Was babbling out of Paradise;
The waters rushing from the rain
Were singing Christ has risen again.
I thought all earthly creatures knelt
From rapture of the joy I felt.
The narrow station-wall's brick ledge,
The wild hop withering in the hedge,
The lights in huntsman's upper storey
Were parts of an eternal glory,
Were God's eternal garden flowers.
I stood in bliss of this for hours.
O glory of the lighted soul.

Silence *Invite the congregation to recall moments when the glory of God, in creation, art, science, music or elsewhere has been real to them.*

Address *A short address can be included here, if required drawing the elements of the service together and expressing the conviction that the glory of God seen chiefly in Jesus is everywhere to be seen and celebrated.*

Hymn Sing we triumphant hymns of praise *(CP 150)*

Affirmation *(The Glory Group. Use different voices in the group for the inset sections)*

Christ is the Lord of the smallest atom,
Christ is the Lord of outer space,
Christ is the Lord of the constellations,
Christ is the Lord of every place:
    Of the furthest star,
    Of the coffee bar,
    Of the length of the Berlin Wall;
    Of the village green,

Of the Asian scene,
Christ is the Lord of all;

Christ is the Lord of the human heart-beat,
Christ is the Lord of every breath,
Christ is the Lord of man's existence,
Christ is the Lord of life and death.

Christ is the Lord of our thoughts and feelings,
Christ is the Lord of all we plan,
Christ is the Lord of a man's decision,
Christ is the Lord of total man:
In the local street,
Where the people meet,
In the church or the nearby hall;
In the factory,
In the family,
Christ is the Lord of all.

Christ is the Lord of our love and courtship,
Christ is the Lord of man and wife,
Christ is the Lord of the things we care for,
Christ is the Lord of all our life.

(Anon)

Hymn   Christ is the world's Light, he and none other

Dismissal

Christ is risen indeed, and goes before you into Galilee.
Your Galilee,
The Galilee of the modern industrial city,
Of the neon lights, and the multiple store,
Where you jostle Christ on the pavement
Among the plate-glass windows.

Galilee Street,
The street in which you live,
And where he waits to move in,
Fulfilling his promise to be with us,
Always,
Even to the end of the world.

Arise, shine,
Thy light is come,
And the glory of the Lord is risen upon thee.

(P. W. Turner)

Acknowledgements

The editor and publishers gratefully acknowledge permission to reproduce the following copyright material:

Quotations from the *New English Bible* 1970 used by permission of the Oxford and Cambridge University Press.

Prayers from *Prayers for the Church Community* used by permission of the National Christian Education Council.

Paragraph from *The Child in the Church* used by permission of the British Council of Churches.

Extract from *A Statement of Faith* used by permission of the Congregational Church in England and Wales.

Rex Chapman:
From *A kind of Praying* used by permission of SCM Press.
Charles Coulson:
Paragraph used by permission of the World Council of Churches.
Rupert Davies:
Poem from *Circles of Community* used by permission of the British Council of Churches.
Caryll Houselander:
Poem from *The Flowering Tree* used by permission of Sheed and Ward.
Mother Julian:
From *Enfolded in Love* by Llewellyn used by permission of Darton Longman and Todd.
John Masefield:
Conversation used by permission of The Society of Authors as the literary representative of the Estate of John Masefield.
Extract from *The Everlasting Mercy* used by permission of The Society of Authors as the literary representative of the Estate of John Masefield.
William Temple:
Extract from a sermon.
P.W.Turner:
Poem from *Christ in the Concrete City* used with permission.

The Festival Service for Palm Sunday was first published in *Partners in Learning* used by permission of the Joint Publications Board.

PRAYERS
FOR
THE CHURCH
COMMUNITY

COMPILED BY

ROY CHAPMAN & DONALD HILTON

A revised reprint of this welcome collection of prayers for those who lead the worship of the Church.

The majority of the prayers included can be used when all age groups are together.

National Christian Education Council
Robert Denholm House
Nutfield, Redhill, Surrey RH1 4HW

Telephone: (0737) 822411 Fax: (0737) 822116